The

Dancing Socrates

and

Other Poems

by

Julian Tuwim

The

DANCING SOCRATES

and

OTHER POEMS

by

JULIAN TUWIM

Selected and Translated

by

ADAM GILLON

Twayne Publishers, Inc., New York

FIRST EDITION

Library of Congress Catalog Card Number 68—57476

MANUFACTURED IN THE UNITED STATES OF AMERICA
BY CZAS PUBLISHING CO., N.Y. N.Y. 11211

For my friend

LUDWIK KRZYŻANOWSKI

ACKNOWLEDGMENTS

The author makes grateful acknowledgment to Mrs. Stefania Tuwim for permission to publish these poems.

Thanks are due to Ludwik Krzyżanowski, editor of *The Polish Review,* in which some of these translations have appeared.

CONTENTS

INTRODUCTION

JULIAN TUWIM was born in Lodz, on September 13, 1894, of middle-class Jewish parents. He was educated there in the Russian Gymnasium (high school), and later studied law and philosophy at the University of Warsaw. His first collection of poems, *Czyhanie na Boga (Lying in Wait for God,* 1918) caused wide controversy, and made him the leader of the *Skamander* literary group. His principal works written before the war were: *Socrates tańczący (The Dancing Socrates,* 1920); *Siódma jesień (The Seventh Autumn,* 1922); *Wierszy tom czwarty (The Fourth Volume of Poems,* 1923); *Słowa we krwi (The Words in Blood,* 1926); *Rzecz Czarnoleska (The Czarnolas Matter,* 1929); *Biblia cygańska i inne wiersze (The Gypsy Bible and Other Poems,* 1933); *Jarmark rymów (The Fair of Rhymes,* 1934); *Treść gorejąca (The Burning Content,* 1936); *Cztery wieki fraszki polskiej (Four Centuries of the Polish Epigram,* 1936); *Lutnia Puszkina (Pushkin's Lute,* 1937); *Lokomotywa i inne wesołe wierszyki dla dzieci (The Locomotive and Other Merry Poems for Children,* 1938).

Tuwim spent the war years in Brazil and the United States, after a short stay in France. *The Polish Flowers* was written while the poet lived in exile. After his return to Poland in 1946 he served as artistic director of *Teatr Nowy* (The New Theatre) and engaged in many literary activities, but although he continued to write poems and translations, no major work came from his pen. It is possible, as some critics claim, that Tuwim's poetry lost some of its vitality after the war. He died suddenly on December 27, 1953 while vacationing in Zakopane.

Tuwim had an immense impact on the Polish language and Polish poetry. As one of the *Skamanderites* he represented the break with the older tradition of national and patriotic themes in poetry. His was a restless, searching talent of which a friend and early mentor (Leopold Staff) spoke thus: "This talent had a hundred colors, a hundred strings; it was always a surprise. There were no small things and big things for Tuwim; he revealed himself in the smallest of things, whole and indivisible. All of him was passion, in the full sense of the word: he was love and suffering. He loved the good, hated the evil, with all his heart.... Today we realize that decades have been waiting for him."

Tuwim's early poetry is marked by an explosive lyricism, and a constant quest for new images and associations. He introduces the urban motif into his poems; he yearns for a fullness of life in all its manifestations. Everything is grist for his poetic mill: the swaying of a branch, the rustling of the wind no less than the anguish of a lover, the despair of the oppressed. He writes of spring, of love, of hatred, of pettiness; he laughs and scorns; he sings and swoons; at all times he is ecstatically conscious of the language he must use to convey the essence of being.

The range of his interests and output was enormous: lyrical poems, philosophical poems and works of social protest, satire, dramatic sketches, popular songs, journalism, translation of great masters from several languages, literary criticism, humorous prose sketches, limericks, aphorisms. He was also a bibliophile, a lexicographer of Bacchic terms, and an anthologist of "literary trifles."

One critic suggested that a Tuwim poem was, as it were, an explosion of a volcano, a series of sudden eruptions of images, poetic ideas, concise summations of thought and emotion. The intensity of Tuwim's early work is illustrated by the frequent mention of *blood.* This word fits neatly into Tuwim's pantheistic view of the world, according to which everything can be deified, everything constitutes an element of God. *Blood* turns into a metaphysical entity which has become flesh, upon which he feeds, which he can drink and breathe, as Tuwim describes it in the poem "The Word and the Flesh" (see p. 35):

> And the Word was made flesh,
> And it has dwelt among us.

The early period of Tuwim's creative work shows an all-embracing optimism, and an exalted notion of poetry which becomes an Epiphany to him:

> Poetry is, hear me gentlemen, a leap,
> A leap of the barbarian who has sensed God. ("Poetry")

10

Poetry, thus, assumes a sacred character. That is why Tuwim sometimes writes poems in the form of a prayer, a litany, or poems evoking the image of Christ. Here he shows some affinity with the Russian symbolist poet, Alexander Blok, whose Christ marches at the head of the rebellious soldiers in "The Twelve." Tuwim speaks of "the Christs of the city." The little man becomes the hero; the sordid city apartment an arena where the whole gamut of human emotions can be displayed. Other Russian writers who influenced Tuwim were Briusov, Balmont and Ivanov. He was also affected by Rimbaud and Walt Whitman. Yet Tuwim is an original poetic genius whose work defies precise classification. One can trace various influences of Russian and European writers but one can also point to his intimate ties with the Polish Renaissance tradition (e.g., the beautiful tribute he pays to Jan Kochanowski in "The Czarnolas Matter," p. 34), with the Polish Romantics like Adam Mickiewicz and Juliusz Słowacki, with the classical tradition (he translated Horace).

Tuwim's mature period starts in the mid-twenties. The poet becomes more reflective and begins to shed his early optimism. A sense of anxiety and horror creeps into his works, especially during the thirties— a time of trial for Tuwim who was savagely attacked by anti-Semitic critics harping on Tuwim's Jewish origins. "Poland did not always love Tuwim," remarked Ilya Ehrenburg, "but Tuwim always loved Poland."

That ardent love for his country is the basic element of *The Polish Flowers,* conceived on a grand scale in the tradition of the Polish epic narrative and the Romantic digressive poem. The projected three parts of the work never materialized, and we have only one volume, or Part One. The book does not quite make it as an epic poem, although it contains some remarkable and moving passages. There is a semblance of plot, but the long poem is primarily an exiled poet's nostalgic examination of his past. Tuwim attempted to present the entire experience of modern Poland through a series of kaleidoscopic recollections and sketches of personal and historical events. Its chief merit lies in the powerful evocation of the poet's anguish as he depicted the rape of Poland by the Nazis, and the shame felt during the thirties

> When a milksop leader, a punk "illumined"
> By the mystic mission straight from Munich
> Wrote for the frightened ministers

11

His epitaph upon the walls,
When the street was ruled
By petty middle-class scoundrels
Who had already turned "Catholics"
But had not yet become Christians . . .

....

When showing toughness they beat the Jews,
When the rampant braggarts so molested them
That I felt more shame for my fatherland
Than pity for my beaten brethren.

Tuwim voices some strong opinions in *The Polish Flowers,* but he had always displayed a violent social consciousness without being, I believe, a political poet *per se.* His genius is lyrical, his temperament that of a sensitive and superb observer, his character—the same he envisaged for the poet: a noble, compassionate soul. Thus it was possible for him to be conservative or extremely radical, since his primary concern, as a poet, was to find the source of the greatest emotion and an opportunity for the fullest self-expression. The best of his poetry is a volcanic eruption, a series of impassioned exclamations, and Tuwim himself is the virtuoso of the language and of life.

*   *   *

I have attempted, where feasible, to render both the prosody and the rhyme scheme of the original. In some cases (e.g., in *The Polish Flowers)* the poem's syllabic structure has been observed. Occasionally, I have tried to approximate the sound of the poem (so important to Tuwim), as in the two poems whose appeal depends on the use of onomatopoeia ("The Two Winds" and "The Train"). In a few translations the rhyme has been left out to ensure a greater accuracy of meaning. In general, my aim has been to identify as closely as possible with the poet's intent, and then to render it in a form which most successfully conveyed the spirit of the poem.

The selections for this book have been made from the five volumes of the still incomplete *Collected Works (Julian Tuwim, Dzieła,* Czytelnik, Warsaw, 1955-1964), but I have consulted several earlier collections. The poems in this volume have been arranged thematically and roughly in a chronological order, except for Part Four.

The Dancing Socrates
and
Other Poems
by
Julian Tuwim

PART ONE

EARLY POEMS

Life

Life?

Relaxing, my arms I shall spread,
And fill my lungs with the morning breeze;

I shall humbly bow to the azure sky,
And shall cry, joyously cry:
How glad I am that my blood is red!

Happiness

I take no interest in the world,
Nor in the great and beauteous cities.
They cannot tell me more than this
Humble roadside weed.

I take no interest in men who
Fathomed every lore.
I'm glad with the first one at my door.
Anybody will do.

About the books I do not give
A rap. You may sneer at my looks,
I know a lot without those books,
And I know what it means to live.

I sat myself under a tree,
Alone I am, serene, in bliss, —
O God, o my happiness!
How shall I give my thanks to Thee?

I

In June at five o'clock in the morning
In the rosy, sunny capital
I walk in the middle of the broadest street,
I walk in the middle of the broadest street!

How bright it is there, and how far
Beyond the bridge, shining across the river!
Ah, how bright it is—how far!

I feel handsome, young and strong!
I'll walk the city, by calm waters I'll stride along,
In the green meadow will I appear,
I'll walk into the distance,
As though drunk on clear
And transparent alcohol.

The Two Winds

One wind—in the field he blew,
Another wind—in the garden grew:
Quietly and very lightly
He caressed the leaves and rustled,
Swooned . . .

One wind—a mighty swell ,
Somersaulted, flatly fell,
Leaped, and surged, soared up high,
Upwards whirled into the sky,
Overturned and dropped pell-mell
Upon a soughing, drowsy garden,
Where so quietly and lightly
Now caressed the leaves and rustled
The other wind.

Off the cherry blossoms flew,
Laughter in all garden grew,
Brother took his twin for friend,
Now they cruise over the land
Chasing clouds and birds in flight,
Rush into the windmill's stance,
And confuse its stupid arms,
Right and left they whistle, dance,
Blow their lungs with all their might,
Clowning in a frenzied riot!

The garden is so quiet . . . quiet . . .

You

You keep me on this earth,
And to the heaven draw near,
You are all to me on this earth,
Why go so far from here?

Today I know but you,
And only you have learned;
I understand no more,
I brushed aside the world.

Each step reveals new roads,
Each thought's a boiling abyss.
You alone reply
In words or a silent kiss.

I hear the blood of your heart,
I feel your misty breath,
And mad with love go on
With this life so full of death.

I'm Nobody's

I'm nobody's in the world,
Nobody's, like a spring or grass;
I'm only yours and God's,
I'm Yours.

I'm only Yours and God's,
Each day I go far off,

Confess to radiant God
My grief.

And I confess in silence,
And silent are my tears,
My God is great silence,
and You...

Each day I await the Coming.
Again to speak of my lament.
And sadly the talk flows
Without words...

My day ends with a prayer;
I recall my radiant dreams...
The remembrance of my God—
—It's You...

Wife

The husband is lazy, a spendthrift, gone astray.
He sits by the window, or runs about town all day.

He watches, watches the tram, the snow, the sky.
He whistles and mutters, he fidgets, snoops like a spy.

He reads voraciously, book after book.
Books and weird papers in every nook.

He babbles nervously; always in a rush.
What's on my husband's mind, what's he saying in a hush?

In the evening he drinks vodka. I'm angry, agog,
In his eyes, dear eyes there's a drunken fog.

In his dear eyes fog... fog in his eye,
But he kneels before me and closes his eyes
And then I understand the word: I.

Death

Like a razor cutting butter, a flash
Through the brain, a stone in water—quiet—splash...

21

Woman

At times she will in rigid numbness freeze,
Horrid, immovable in thoughtless thought;
Dull apathy upon her soul will seize,
And fear, as if she saw a dead mouse rot.

With agony her glassy eyes are blind,
Of chaos full, and sad infinitude,
And crumpled thoughts come thick upon her mind,
And fields in madness throng, and deserts brood.

Wake her, and drunk with chaos she will start,
As though she had *returned:* yet hides much more,
For when she hoarsely speaks, her words impart
She has remained a savage, as of yore.

Oldsters

We watch the streets, the gutters
Through half-open shutters.

We kiss strange children's heads,
And water window flower-beds.

We live, accept God's wages,
We tear off calendar pages.

Search

Three men—smiling and calm. Polite.
"Oh, yes ... And here?They ferret and feel ...
(The corners of their mouths—what fright,
And their eyes—the points of faithless steel).

One, uniformed, reads on his knee.
Faded, as if dully sad—but lies—
The other. Through the fearful glass you see
The third one's eyes, a sleuth's rat eyes.

This? Move that? Please! (Deep inside
Something falls moaning—lasting pain ...)
Cold fear reels ... A little word has died—
He's drawn it out ... Hm ... So ... Explain ..."

Litany

O God, I ardently pray
O God, I heartily pray,
For the injury of the humiliated,
For the trembling of those who wait,
For eternal non-return of the dead,
For the helplessness of the dying,
For the sadness of the misunderstood,
For men hopelessly begging,
For those insulted, ridiculed,
For the stupid, the evil and the petty,
For those who rush breathlessly
To the nearest doctor,
For those who come home
From the city, with their hearts beating,
For those rudely jostled,
For those hissed off the stage,
For boring, ugly, clumsy people,
For weak, beaten, oppressed men,
For those who cannot fall asleep,
For those who fear the coming of death,
For people waiting in pharmacies,
For those who miss their trains,
—FOR ALL THE DWELLERS OF THE WORLD,
For their troubles and sorrows,
Their worries, mishaps, afflictions,
Their anxiety, and anguish,
The yearning and adversity,
For every throbbing
That is not happiness or joy
Which should shine upon these men
Forever, with loving kindness—
O God, I ardently pray,
O God, I heartily pray.

Our Wisdom

How shall I teach you this wisdom then?
We're quiet men, we're simple men.

We're simple men, untaught,
Christened by word-fire, by word-fire wrought.

Our tangled words grasp mystery in tuneful rhyme.
The flower's called sun, flower is sun's name.

But in our speech, in this most wondrous wonder, this
Our world is called as it really is.

Without books, without learning we sit
In dumb thought. We alone know a little bit:

About those nightly minutes, running, never caught,
When we see the shadows of we know not what.

We always remain young on the earth,
A bright Herald walks our garden paths.

And till our death we render humbly
Unto God what's Caesar's, unto God what's godly.

The Dancing Socrates

I roast in the sun, old wretch...
I lie, and yawn, I stretch.
Old am I, but full of pep:
When I take a slug from the cup
I sing.

My ancient bones bask in the sun's glow,
And my curly, wise, gray head.
In that wise head, like woods in spring
Hums and hums a wiser wine.
Eternal thoughts flow and flow,
Like time.

Hey, Cyrbeus, why do you gape?
What d'you think? The old fool has said
His last, has no more words to scrape?
Yes... yes.... Go, bake your bread.

From the alley the students mock;
Their master's flipped his lid.
Socrates is drunk...
Go, Cyrbeus, tell that kid
That I have hit the mark;
That virtue is all bunk;
To lick the dust off an Athenian street!
Or tell'em virtue is blowing a bladder!
That virtue's filling jugs with water!
Or spilling it!—it doesn't matter...
And if you wish—sit at my feet,
Don't bake your horns and rolls.
We'll take another cup,
Come, bottoms up!

Are you embarrassed, hey
Cyrby, that I'm confused, stepped out of line?
That I laugh so much? That in broad day
I lie in Athens' market, sipping wine,
Beggar-like? It ill befits a wiseman, you say,
To set such a bad example for his students?
The old man babbles
Like children.
No longer do I address
Throngs of disciples, nor point the way
To wisdom, give advice,
Nor philosophize...
Yes... Oh, yes....

Evil and good!—truth?—gods and men,
Eternity, virtue, the word and the deed,
And from the beginning once again,
Evil and good, gods and men,
Words and deeds, the Republic's needs,
Beauty this, and beauty that!—
My friend—it's a joke.
You've heard from Herifon
That I'm the wisest... Thus spoke
The oracle in all of Greece revered;
The lustre of fame adorns my brow!
Look then, what the wisest man does now:
Oh!
For what's a word and what's a deed,
And what's good, and what's evil,
When I got drunk on a golden wine,
And a shaggy canine head is mine,
And my head is filled with maddening fancy?
Look how your philosopher is dancing!
How his old legs leap and prance,
Good and evil, gods and men,
Virtue, truth, eternal moira,
Yippy yeah, yippy oyra,
Once to your right—yippy yeah!

Once to your left—yippy yeah!
Yippy rippin', come Xanthippe!
Let the music play!

Come you too dear fellow Cyrby,
Hop with me around the market;
The philosopher is dancing,—off with
Virtue, truth and gods and beauty.
Look ye people, look ye gapers,
I'll be trounced by my Xanthippe,
Everything is throbbing in me,
But I keep on, yippy yeah!
Thus without an end, till death calls
Let the brilliant sky keep spinning,
Upward so—and kicking downward,
Sideways, yippy yeah and running,
Pity not the ancient legs!
Let the potent God rejoice:
Socrates does know the truth,
Yes, he does! And has it all!
To the very brink he's gone away
The chosen one—the most advanced,
The rascal with an ugly snout
Has learned the dance, has learned the dance.
Yippy yeah and yippy yeah.

PART TWO

THE MATURE PERIOD

O, words! Sharp and golden!
Pouncing words of prey,
Like lions! Like lions!

More About the Past

My palm over closed eyes—
—Like the poet of a childish vision—
Now I myself
Am a poet,
Myself almost holy,
Persist in non-remembrance,
Cut out of the youthful dream
As if from tissue paper,
Light am I,
Gently whisper words,
Drum my fingers on my forehead.

Thus it was in those loving, lazy mornings:
The lily-colored image throbbed in my eyes.
Thus in a dark mailman's bag
Lovers' letters could encounter.
Like what?
Just like this:
This childish thought about the poet
With a bow of the poet's graying head.

Poem

When I know
that a poem
will arise,
I lock the world
in the bracket's vise
and before the bracket place
a symbol
of factor, equation.

Then begins the calculation,
sonorous and quick contemplation
until the poem,
like the problem
of an algebraist,
clearly follows on the blackboard.

Then
from the bracket I release
the imprisoned elements, remove
the calculation off the board
and come home, seized
with joy, back from school,
but at home I die of love.

Request for a Song

If, O God, I have Thy splendid gift, the Word,
Cause my heart to beat with the wrath of oceans;
Give me the ancient poets' noble sword,
To strike at the tyrants with raging emotions.

No need for hymns to throng my head
To sing the wasted man, of an empty heart,
Ready to supplicate for a bit of bread,
Who for the king must play his menial part.

Give my angry words the flash of steel,
A fantasy and rhyme—well-aimed and strong,
So that the targets I shall hit feel
The sharp rapier of my glittering song.

Draw Blood With the Word!

Your words are like drawing room doggies
And mine—are rabid dogs!
To heck with your arabesques and burlesques,
And—instead of placing dots and dashes,—
Slap faces in your poems,
Slam your fists into mugs!
Tear up, rip into bits
Your sonnets, tintinnabulation,
Fools!
Let the languid, flaxen-haired
And lustful maidens
Grow to hate all poetry!
Let the word draw blood—as a meatcleaver
Hits the head!
O, words! Sharp and golden!
Pouncing words of prey!
Pouncing words of prey,
Like lions! Like lions!

My Theme

My theme—is transformation,
Change and fermentation,
Being consumed in a fiery flight,
Coalescing into a drop of light,
Into love's elation.

My theme—the thing's to reach zenith in strife,
Neither death nor life.
The last one, pure, the motherly fuss,
It stays transparent as centuries pass,
A dot upon the summit's knife.

33

With the Crumbs of Youth

With the crumbs of youth—what shall one do? Cast them to the birds?
One can both cast them to the birds and put them into words.
They will fly away, gladdened, to return for more,
Both words, and birds—with hope winged alike, will come as before.

And what will you tell them? There is no more! You'll tell the poor ones,
there's no more.
Will they believe? No, they won't. They will wait
Behind the window till the cloudy night grows late,—
They'll strike the panes with wings. The birds
Will fall, dead and true. Both birds and words.

The Czarnolas*Matter

The Czarnolas heritage surges,
Surrounds, stirs with wonder him who
Is possessed. The word slowly emerges,
Changing in sound, is real, true.

From chaos form, necessity,
Oneness of moment when the immensity
Itself of the creative frame
Finds its finality, calls its name.

Deaf unreason, darkling human sense,
Shot through and through with the sharp ray,
Wakened and released by the breath
Of the great Rennaisance lay.

---

* *Czarnolas* (literally Darkwood) — a small estate of Jan Kochanowski (1530-84), greatest Polish Renaissance poet, where he composed his greatest masterpieces (e.g., *Laments, Psalter);* hence the symbol of poetic inspiration and excellence.

The Word and the Flesh*

I

And the Word was made flesh,
And it has dwelt among us,
I feed the starving body
With words as if they were fruit;
I drink the words with my mouth,
Swallow them like cold water,
I breathe them like brilliant air,
Crush them like little young leaves,
I grind them with sweet odors.

The word is wine and honey,
The word is meat and it's bread,
It's the word that guides my eye
Along the starry sky.
O joy of the sacred gift,
O eternal fondness!
O Lord, grant me today
My common word!

II

I have no occupation:
I'm only a hunter of words,
Watchful and attentive,
I've gone to hunt into the world.

With words the minutes flow,
And everything I love and felt
Buzzes around as the days go—
A swarm of sunny bees.

* A reference to St. John, I, 14.

35

They caress me with their wings,
Their stingers draw my blood.
I'm stung by poisoned words,
I feel so good!

Enclosed within my heart
The words are a-flutter.
That's why the heart trembles so.
My head is drunk
On a charmed honey;
That's why—the dreams.

The Gypsy Bible

What is the gypsy bible like?
Unwritten, wandering, prophetic.
Whispered to hags by the silver night,
Illumined by midsummer moon.

It bears the aroma of crushed myrtle,
The rustling of woods, the starred cabala,
Graveyard's shadow, deck of cards,
Churchdoor beggar, white chimera.

Who found this book? We, the learned ones
Who search the junkyard of remembrance,
Driven by scent, and touched by portent,
Gazing beneath the senses and thought.

Along the valleys of fallen knowledge
The twisted myth flows river-like:
Not in life nor death but in between,
Witching for death, enchanting for life.

Funeral tapers trickle waxen
Tears at night upon this volume.
In this book the dreams turn over
Like pages, moved by delusive guesses.

The flashing verses whirl about,
You won't grasp what they conceal, as
It were: the poet's martyrdom . . .
. . . something he must save . . . .

The book melts away.

To the Common Man

When they begin to plaster walls
With freshly printed proclamations,
When "to the people," and "to soldiers"
Black print will sound alarm
And any punk or any mobster
Believes in their eternal lie
That one must go and fire cannons,
Must murder, poison, burn and plunder,
When they start clawing at the Fatherland
In thousandfold variations,
Deceive with colored emblems,
With "history's right" incite to action
For expansion, glory, border,
Forefathers, fathers and the flag,
For heroes and for victims;
When the bishop, pastor, rabbi
Goes out to bless your rifle,
Because the Lord has whispered to him
"One must fight for Fatherland;"
When the clamor of daily headlines
Has grown bitchy and brutish
And a horde of howling hags tosses
Flowers upon the "little soldiers."—
—O my unlearned friend,
My kin of this or any other land!
You'll know it's the kings, the bulging
Lords who toll the bells for danger,
You'll know it's for the birds, mere fraud,
When they command you "Shoulder weapon!"
It means that somewhere they struck oil
Which bore a progeny of dollars;
That something is awry in banks they own,
Or that somewhere they sniffed full registers,
Or the bloated shysters now concocted

A higher duty for their cotton.
Throw your rifle to the pavement!
The blood is yours, and theirs is but oil!
And from one capital to another
Cry out in defense of your hard-earned bread:
"Gentlemen,—tell that to the marines!"

A Ball at the Opera
(Fragments)

I

Today's the Grand Opera Ball.
The omnipotent Archdictator
Gave his supreme protectorate.
All the sluts wash their panties
And buy their clothes on credit,
Throngs and traffic jams in the street,
Soldiers muster for the parade,
Pancer cavalry helmets glow,
Polished officer boots glisten,
Horses foam and neigh,
Cars roar, crowds surge.
In the *corps de garde* troops like ants,
State of readiness everywhere,
Impatient wines sparkle,
At the hairdressers' people faint
Waiting for their turn.
Sluts' calves tremble sweetly.

II

From their towers the astronomers,
Their eyes upon the starry expanse,
Saw a miracle in their telescopes:

Apes ran across the firmament!
In the zodiacal merry-go-round
Reigns apocalyptic turmoil.
At the stands of earlier beasts
Twelve ugly apes took their seats,
And began to plant the ape misrule
Amidst the planetary voids.
The wicked monkeys spun the wheel
Of heavens into a mad dance;
They leap, they run about and prance as
Behind the metal bars of their cage
They display the plump reddish bottoms to
The earth. No more celestial portents!
The ape now orbits in the zodiac!
And like a weighty nightmare he now
Hangs over this awesome starry night,
Orders the constellations to dance
When the devils take the monkeys,
The devils take, the devils shall take!

Mother

I

At the cemetery in Lodz
The Jewish cemetery, stands
The Polish grave of my mother,
My Jewish mother's tomb.

The grave of my Mother, the Pole,
Of my Mother the Jewess;
I brought her from land over Vistula
To the bank of industrial Lodz.

A rock fell on the tombstone,
Upon the face of the pale rock
A few laurel leaves
Shed by a birch tree.

And when a sunny breeze
Plays with them a golden game,
The leaves are patterned into
The Order of Polonia.

II

A fascist shot my mother
When she was thinking of me;
A fascist shot my mother
When she was longing for me.

He loaded—killed the longing,
Again began to load,
So that later... but later
There was nothing left to kill.

41

He shot through my mother's world:
Two tender syllables;
Threw the corpse out the window
Upon the holy pavement.

Remember well, little daughter!
Recall this, future grandson!
The word has come true:
"The ideal reached the pavement."

I took her from the field of glory,
Returned to mother-earth...
But the corpse of my name
Still lies buried there.

PART THREE

THE POLISH FLOWERS

My song born in defeat and anguish,
Huge serpent reared beyond the seas,
You rose from flowers, motley, twisted,
You will turn into flowers again.

The Polish Flowers

(Fragments)

1

And you, Warsaw dogs, on judgment day
Fulfill your canine duty—
Howl yourselves into a running pack
To wreak fierce vengeance for your victims.
For dogs torn by exploding bombs,
That perished under the shattered home,
For those which howled over their master,
As they scratched his lifeless hands; and for
Dogs that exercised a hopeless charm
To curry favor with dead bodies;
For the death of puppies still at play
In their basket in the basement;
And for dogs desperately running,
For those deserted in apartments,
Gasping for breath in smoke, half-alive,
Remembering their kindly ladies;
For growling dogs, and those believing
In man's return since dogs were waiting.
And thus, the trusting dog sat upon
A man's grave in a waiting pose;
For the imploring look in the eyes
Scared by the tumult, crash and fires,
For the dogs which tore the ground with nails
Digging their shelters in the gardens,—
For all the miseries and troubles,
Suffered by you and those who loved you
Amidst these common walls and ruins,
Howl, o my brothers, come to Dog's Field!
Let rabid foam rise in your muzzles,
Loose the breathless pack in hot pursuit
Of the German trail, when they scuttle
From Poland, with only their breeches!

Sharpen your fangs on bricks of rubble,
And on the whitened human bones;
And when you get them—leap at their throats,
You mastiffs, leap at their gullets,
Sink your sharp fangs and tear away
Before the rascals' final rattle!
To their Adam's apples, she-volves! Claws
Into their eyes, before they twinkle!
Let the armies of the lesser dog-
Avengers fall on them when they're down,
Tear them to bits so that even their
Mothers never shall know where to look
For their parts, scattered over the earth...!

For ours could not find them either,
Their babies' heads, little legs and fists...

2

                     To get an answer
The author went to Antipodes.
He also knew in Poland, of course,
But had not known how hard it would come

5   Down on him while he was free and young,
The other side of the Great Water.
Far away, across the Vistula,

L. 2. *to Antipodes* — e.g., to the point on the other side of the globe.
L. 6. *The Other side of the Great Water* — beyond the ocean, in America, where
Tuwim stayed while writing parts of this poem.

Where the crow "wasbathing"
Did the captain know
10 It was his wife;
Captain, Sir, a word:
It's not your wife,—
It's just a bird
Called a crow ...
15 For this little folksong, this one too,
Is unique, and is inevitable.
Wherever carried by any sails,
Though your land is far, it's always near ...
A fatherland is Scent—suddenly:
20 Smoke in the field, without the fire
In sight. + A low white cottage huddles
In a cherry garden. + In the swamp
The will o'the wisp at night. + Corner
Of Traugutt and Mazovietzka streets.
25 And how's your health, my dear flowergirl? +
How far is it to Redultov Road?
Half a mile, go that-a-way, not far.
+ The smell of a wet harness. + Horses.
Steaming into the frost. + "Dear lady!
30 People are so..." + In the train early
In the morning yellow-skinned, sleepless
Passengers. + A castle in misty
Frost. + "Shall I spray with vegetalis?"

L. 7-14. A quotation from a well-known Polish folksong.
L. 19. Here Tuwim begins a veritable catalogue of objects and popular sayings that remind him of his land.
L. 23-24. *Corner of Traugutt* — in Warsaw where Tuwim lived on Mazowiecka Street before the War.
L. 33. *vegetalis* — hair spray.

+ Carts loaded with coal have entered our
35 Little yard. Unloading. + Carnival
Dawn greets "Oasis." + Stalls at the Green
Market in Lodz. + Dill in the pickle jar. +
At the door of Simon's Restaurant
Taxicabs. + A village funeral
40 Along a path; they're singing. + In a
Car, through the Avenue rides Piłsudski
In gray and blue. + Night. Prince Joseph in
Hoary frost. + Dawn over Vistula. +
45 Sheep bleating at Kalatov meadows. +
Easter lambs in window displays. + On
Christmas Eve latecomers carry trees
To their homes. + Yellow water lilies
Over greenish water. + Barefoot with
50 A shroud over his head, a shepherd
Soaking wet in the field. + A little
Silver coffin in the window, with
An obituary. + Scribbled notes:
"Room with family . . ." + Hortensia glass.
55 Wedel chocolate. + Quarter cuts of meat,
Marked by blue pencil, hanging from a
Hook. + Great review in a movie house

L. 36. *Oasis* — name of a restaurant.
L. 40. *Avenue* — Aleje Ujazdowskie — Warsaw's Champs-Elysées.
L. 41. *Piłsudski* — Marshal Joseph Piłsudski (1867-1935), first head of the Polish republic, subsequently premier (1926-1928, 1930) and undisputed military ruler of Poland.
L. 42. *gray and blue* — a reference to the uniform Piłsudski wore.
L. 42. *Prince Joseph* — a monument of Prince Joseph Poniatowski (1763-1813), a Polish general who fought the Russians, in Warsaw.
L. 45. *Kalatov* (Kalatówki) — in the Tatra mountains.
L. 54. *Hortensia* — glass works in Piotrków; *Wedel* — well-known chocolate and candy manufacturing firm.

at Wola. + Petty advertisements
In "Warsaw Courier" (each a story
60 By Prus the interiors of the flats). +
Across the Praga Bridge, and New Drive
In a droshky. + Birthday of Leszek.
Market Lane, Fret's Street. + Under the stalls
Old women squat on pavements selling
65 Dried herbs. "He will not pass along
Moniuszko street." + Villanowa Park
On a sunny October morning;
A copper fire of leaves. + Fish in
The shops at the crossing of Hoza
70 And Mokotov streets. + "Window panes—panes!"
(Glazier, old Jew.) + Visitation Church
In the moonlight. + Friend Nina Morsztyn.
Vodka at noon at Plavovitz place. +
Sikorz flowers. + Suppleness of birch

L. 59. *Warsaw Courier* — a newspaper established in 1821, which appeared before the war. *Prus* — Bolesław Prus, pseudonym of Alexander Głowacki (1847-1912), a Positivist novelist, renowned for his vignettes of city life.
L. 62. *Leszek* — Jan Lechoń (1899-1956), pseudonym of Leszek Serafinowicz, poet, member of the Skamander Group to which Tuwim belonged.
L. 63. Lechoń lived in this district during his youth.
L. 71. *Visitation Church* in the Cracow Boulevard (Krakowskie Przedmieście) in Warsaw.
L. 72. *Nina Morsztyn* — wife of the writer Ludwik Hieronimo Morstin, a friend of Tuwim.
L. 73. *Plavovitz* — Pławowice, an estate of the Morstins, which Tuwim visited at times.
L. 74. *Sikorz* — An estate of the Plawickis, near Otwock. Tuwim used to spend his vacations there in the late thirties. In the summer of 1936 he wrote "A Ball at the Opera" while at there.

75 Twigs (can twist into a knot). + A smith
Shoeing a horse, the peasant holding
The bridle. + The flickering lights in
Village huts when travelling by train
On a winter evening. + A little
80 Horse pulls a pine tree through the forest
Path; the wheels creak; the peasant lowered
His feet. + "Distribution" at Soltz. "What's
That? You're saying, mister?" + Mangles.
(Sign: a jacketed corpse turning a wheel.)
85 + "Tickets p... please..." Suddenly a flock of
Pigeons flew off the Mariatzki Church
Tower. + "We're poor but we have a ball."
"Main thing's not to worry..." "Hey, you nut,
Vistula's on fire." + Tart taste of
90 Sorb-trees. + Tiny Podhale churches
Dark and wooden. + The Commissariat
On Saturday evening. + "Is it fit
For a wench so?" + I do not go to
The Malinowskis: drafts..." + "Chocolate,
95 Newspapers, beer, lemonade!" + "S..., I
Tell y'a man (said with a Lvov accent)."
+ Break Hungarian plums. + Artificial
Flowers, and gorgeous wreaths by Makart.
Wieniawa's face swollen from weeping,
100 When upon a prancing horse he leads
The marshal's funeral. Visiting
Wawel a few days before the war...

L. 82. *"Distribution"* — a give-away.
L. 86. *Mariatzki* — Mariacki Church in Cracow.
L. 87-89. Warsaw street sayings.
L. 98. Hans *Makart* (1840-1884) — that is in his highly decorative style.
L. 99. Bolesław Wieniawa Długoszowski (1881-1942) Piłsudski's adjutant; translated Baudelaire in his youth; old friend of Tuwim.
L. 102. *Wawel* — famous castle in Cracow.

3

And then—
Then divide all this and me by the
Atlantic of yearning. Afterwards
Multiply by this Atlantic and
The yearning a hundred times! A thousand!
No, a thousand-and-one! There will be
Folktales of Scheherazade which once
Sustained our daily life, which we breathed,
Unaware that every moment we
Breathed the air of myths! That Lodz
Is legendary Baghdad city
Or Manchester-like La-Mancha,
Tomaszov, oh, ageless Toboso,
That Warsaw is heroic Troy, and
Jerusalem before whose walls two
Peoples now lament, and sing a
Gloomy song of one misfortune...
Who then could know that Cracow would turn
Into a distant, holy Mecca,
Mount Gievont—turned the Seventh Mountain,
And Vistula—the Seventh River?
My country is my home.* Fatherland
Is my home. My lot was to receive
A Polish home. This—is fatherland,
And other countries are hotels.
My home. Apartment. Room. A desk,
In it (remember?) that drawer
Where over the years one put away
Old wallets no longer in use,

* Tuwim uses the original English here.

Dated receipts and calling cards, the
Remains of a bulb, quarter pencils...
The drawer contains a cuff link, pipe,
Screw, an empty Syndeticone tube,
Some tweezer or an eye dropper,
And aged, tattered money purse,
Gambling dice, a little cork of glass,
A cancelled railway ticket stub,
A little chamois case, a dried out
Tiny brush, a small medallion,
Sealing wax, a lizard letter weight
Without its tail, expired pass;
A brown fountain pen engraved in white
"Zakopane," a crank for something,
A key to something—both items good
For nothing. In short, you know this drawer...
When you examine its inside well,
You'll find there your little fossilized
Heart which you lost amidst old rubbish...
Hence don't throw out a thing, don't clear...
Useful or not—leave it alone.
Spare the rubbish when you arrange
Such drawers and nooks, for you have shared
A bit of your life with every thing.
You last,—not knowing, with all this junk...
This drawer is like your fatherland:
You can throw out nothing. You cannot
Ransack the storehouse of affection
And remove "the needless," "the unused."
Let it remain with you. You say this
Is but superstition? Yes, indeed ...
The learned men call it—a myth
And from this daily mythology
Of sudden, back-street apparitions,
Dazzlements, from color, line and tune
A moment will become fatherland.

It will appear indubitable,
So exclusive, not to be faked,
That you will know it from the echo,
Will sense it from its very shadow:
This is it—this is your own, alive.

4

We are modest men, we're simple men,
No supermen, nor any giants.
We ask our God for a different might,
For another road to greatness:

(The Prayer)*

Kindle the clouds into a glare, and
Strike at our hearts with a bell of gold,
Open our Poland as with a bolt
You clear up the overcast heavens.
Allow us to rid our fathers' home
Of our cinders, and holy ruins:
Let our house be poor but also clean,
Our house, raised from the cemetery.
To the land, when it stirs from the dead,
And is gilded by freedom's luster,
Give the rule of wise and righteous men,
Mighty in wisdom and in goodness.

---

* This fragment won acclaim as an independent poem. It was widely circulated in
hand-written copies in occupied Poland during the last war, under the title "Prayer,"
and it gave hope to many Polish readers.

And when the people rise to their feet,
Let them raise their veiny, calloused fists:
Give the toilers ownership, the fruit
Of their labor in villages and
Cities. Chase away the bankers, Lord,
Stop the growth of money from money.
Let the vain be armed with humbleness,
To the humble give an angry pride.
Teach us that under Your sunny sky
"There is no more Greek and no more Jew."
Knock the stupid crown from the heads of
Puffed up men and the supercilious.
And set up the skull of a dead man
On the desk of a growling ruler.
Strike with your bolt when in glory's name
A haughty man seizes his weapon,
Do not permit an unjust sword to
Have for a handle the cross of Your
Agony. Let good-will be done, of
Noble hearts which grew up in defeat.
Give us back the bread of Polish fields,
Return the coffins of Polish pine,
But above all give our words, altered
Craftily by wheelers and dealers,
Their uniqueness and their truthfulness:
Let the law always denote law, and
Let justice mean nothing but justice.
Let more of Your name resound in deeds
Of men than in their song; take away
The gift of dreaming from the stupid,
Realize the dreams of noble men.

Cause us to bless the conflagration
That destroyed our property, if it
Proves to be a purifying fire
For our souls touched with decay. Any
Size of Poland—let her have greatness:
To the sons of her spirit or her
Body give a greatness of hearts if
She's great, and a greatness of hearts
If she's small. Wedged between the German
Barbarian and the new nation of
A hundred nations—give a friendly
Frontier on the east, an eternal
Abyss on the west. Tear off the cross
Your hands that bleed, together with nails,
And cover, cover Your eyes with them
When the time of vengeance draws near us,
Give us leave to break Your commandment,
When we wade toward Warsaw across
The Tatra Mountains of dead Germans,
The Baltic of enemy's damned blood.
... When we approach O Necropolis
Your suburbs, in a quarantine we
Will kneel in the field, full of hope and
Anguish: hope—that friends shall come to meet
Us from the City of the Crosses,
Bearing forgiveness in their eyes and
Tears of happiness not a reproach.
Anguish—that these tears, this kindness and
These greetings shall be of no avail...
THE SILENT THING between us shall rise—
A dreadful phantom.

Poetry! What's your name? Creative?
What do you create? Yourself. You are
A tinder-box—a fire—and a smoke—
Your golden crop shines in the sowing,
Of seed cast into the darkness—a
Fallout of shooting stars. Thus I run
Into the night to gather the stars.
They aren't there. Only a glowing trail
Will remain in my eyes—the falling:
You are a star and its very trail.
O goblet which in its being is
Wine already, intoxication,
And drunken song as well, thereafter
Returns to its own shape in a dream.
Then—it's a memory of this dream.
I raise you high my secret goblet,
My fire, bountiful sowing of stars,
You, who are a goal and a reason,
You, the firstness and finality!
Drinking wine in a toast to wine, I
Extol through you my eternity.

O Poetry! This toast is for my
Jubilee. It is thirty years now
Since you brought to me the first news, on
That radiant night—misty today. And
Since that time, Adam and Orpheus,
In Eden or in hell—in your grip—
I visit heights and precipices . . .
Ten thousand days and ten thousand nights
Or, let us be precise: eleven.
For to whom shall I give—a thousand?
I cannot spare a single hour,
A minute—not even a minute:
Thus I believe in you, when I kiss,
Thus I sweetly suffer when in doubt.

6

As the magician draws from the depths
Of his top hat many-colored scarves,
Roses which he throws to the ladies,
A pair of rabbits or white pigeons,
A glass of wine—so in this manner
Enchanted by word's magic oath I
Draw the flowered ribbons of the days
From my memory's double bottom,
From the Lethean depth of my heart . . .

PART FOUR

POEMS FOR CHILDREN

What do you sing, incomprehensible
Little creature, seized by madness?
Your song lists ancient animals—
Why do you give them diminutive names?
What devil runs amok within you?
It's not a doggie—but a Terrible Dog!

—From "A Poem Sneering at Children"

The Train*

A locomotive stands at the station,
Heavy, enormous, drips perspiration:
Greasy oil.

She stands, gasping, panting and blowing,
The heat from her boiling belly glowing:
BANG how hot it is!
CLANG how hot it is!
PUFF how hot it is!
HUFF how hot it is!

She barely puffs and holds her soul,
But the stoker still fills her with coal;
They hitched to her railroad cars,
Big and heavy, of iron bars,
And lots of people here and farther,
In one stand horses—cows in another;
Fat men only sit in the third;
They eat thick sausage without a word.
The fourth one carries a load of bananas,
In the fifth there stand six grand pianos.
In the sixth a cannon, of heavy steel,
An iron beam beneath each wheel.
In the seventh oaken tables, a chest and chair,
An elephant in the eighth, giraffes, a bear.
The ninth has only fattened pigs,
In the tenth are parcels, boxes and rigs,
And forty cars are in the train,
I cannot tell what else they contain.
But even though a thousand athletes came,
Each having had a thousands steaks on the road,

* The original reads *Lokomotywa* (Locomotive).

58

And each engaged his mighty frame,
They could not budge the heavy load.

Then—a hiss!
Then—a whizz!
The steam—bang!
The wheels—clang!
At first she's slow

          like a turtle,

               and fettered,

She moves on the rails

          with a sluggish

                clatter.
She tugs at the cars and pulling with strain,
She's turning and turning the wheels of the train.
She gathers some speed and she goes now much faster,
She echoes, she rattles, and speed is her master.
But whereto? But whereto? But whereto? Ahead!
On the rails, on the rails, on the bridge she sped;
Through tunnels and mountains and woods she must climb,
She hurries and hurries to get there on time.
She clatters and raps click—clickety—clickety,
Clickety—clickety—clickety—clickety.
Smoothly so, slightly so, does she now roll,
As if she were merely a tiniest ball.
It's not an exhausted and panting machine
But rather a plaything, a toy made of tin.

And where is she speeding so, why such a rush?
And who is it pushing and why all this rush?
Why does she hurtle and boom, bang, bang!?
It's steam that's hot, that has set her to clang,
The steam from the boiler to piston is piped,
And pistons then activate wheels on two sides,
They run and they push and they keep the train rolling,
The steam is still pumping the pistons, not stalling.
And wheels are a-clatter, and rapping click-clickety,
Clickety-clack, click, clickety-clickety . . . .

The Turnip[*]

Gramps has planted a turnip in the yard;
Every day he goes to see it and guard.
The turnip has grown huge—a juicy spread,
He'd like to eat it with some bread.
Poor granpa pulls, but it's a losing bout.
He pulls, and pulls but *cannot* pull it out.
He called, "Hey, Granny, come over and see.
I shall grab the turnip, and you grab me."
Now granpa and granma huff and they pout,
They pull and pull but *cannot* pull it out.

Granny tugs at granpa's pants.
Gramps over the turnip bends,
Would they had another pair of hands!
They sweat and huff, they groan and pout,
They pull, and pull but *cannot* pull it out.

Johnny came, ready to give a fight.
He sweats, and groans, o what a sight!
Johnny holds his granny's apron strings,
Granny to granpa's pants still clings,
Granpa over the turnip bends,
Would they had another pair of hands!
They sweat and huff, they groan and pout,
They pull, and pull but. *cannot* pull it out.

Then Johnny called his puppy Grumbles;
Grumbles ran to him quick, in tumbles.
Grumbles holds on to his master tight,
Johnny pulls Granny with all his might,
Granny tugs at Granpa's pants,
Granpa over the turnip bends,

[*] After an old Russian tale.

60

Would they had another pair of hands!
They sweat, and huff, they groan and pout.
They pull, and pull but *cannot* pull it out.
Kitty was stalking a hen named Gritty.
Grumbles barked: "Please, help us, Kitty!"
Kitty now pulls at Grumbles,
Grumbles fumbles with Johnny's shirt,
Johnny holds on to his granma's skirt,
Granny tugs at granpa's pants,
Granpa over the turnip bends,
Would they had another pair of hands!
They sweat, they huff, they groan and pout,
They pull, and pull but *cannot* pull it out.

So Kitty   called upon hen Gritty.
Gritty came running from the yard.
Gritty pulls at Kitty hard,
Kitty pulls at Grumbles' tail,
Grumbles pulls at Johnny's shirt,
Johnny pulls at Granny's skirt,
Granny tugs at Granpa's pants,
Granpa over the turnip bends,
Would they had another pair of hands!
They sweat, they huff, they groan and pout,
They pull, and pull but *cannot* pull it out.

Then came a flock of geese.
Gritty said: "Oh help us, please!"
One goose grabbed the wing of Gritty,
Gritty pulls the tail of Kitty,
Kitty pulls at Grumbles' tail,
Grumbles pulls at Johnny's shirt,
Johnny pulls at Granny's skirt,
Granny tugs at Granpa's pants,
Granpa over the turnip bends,
Would they had another pair of hands!

They sweat, they huff, they groan and pout,
They pull, and pull, but *cannot* pull it out.

Long-nosed Stork was flying high.
"Storky, help us, fly here, fly!"
Storky grabbed white goose's thigh,
The goose pulls hen Gritty,
Gritty pulls the tail of Kitty,
Kitty pulls at Grumbles' tail,
Grumbles pulls at Johnny's shirt,
Johnny pulls at Granny's skirt,
Granny tugs at Granpa's pants,
Granpa over the turnip bends.
Would they had another pair of hands!
They sweat, they huff, they groan and pout,
They pull, and pull but *cannot* pull it out.

Along came a little greenish frog.
He grabbed the stork and not the dog!
Little Froggy drags and drags,
Storky pulls the goose's legs,
The goose pulls hen Gritty,
Gritty pulls the tail of Kitty,
Kitty pulls at Grumbles' tail,
Grumbles pulls at Johnny's shirt,
Johnny pulls at Granny's skirt,
Granny tugs at granpa's pants,
Granpa pulls the turnip with his hands.
Then the jackdaw also came,
For she had an eye upon the same
Enormous turnip, and she dragged
The little frog by his hind leg.

All strained together
Muscle and feather,
Joined in this mighty bout.
Suddenly—crash! The turnip's *out!*
It's simply a shame to tell
How next they all fell
One on top of the other:—

The turnip onto Granpa's knee,
Granpa on Grandmother,
Granny on little Johnny,
Johnny on Grumbles,
Grumbles on Kitty tumbles,
Kitty on hen Gritty,
Gritty on the goose lies,
The goose at Storky flies,
Falling like a log,
Storky on the little frog,
The frog upon the jackdaw, and
At the very end
The jackdaw fallen thus
Upon the grass.